the **after**life ~

ROBERT BOATES

the **after**life ~

ROBERT BOATES

Seraphim Editions

Published in 1998 by
Seraphim Editions
970 Queen Street East
P.O. Box 98174
Toronto, Ontario
Canada M4M 1J0

Canadian Cataloguing in Publication Data

Boates, Robert, 1954—
The Afterlife

Originally published: Hamilton, Ont.: Hamilton Haiku Press, 1992.

Poems.
ISBN 0-9699639-4-7

1. Title.

PS8553.038A75 1998 C811'.54 C98-900730-8
PR9199.3.B63A65 1998

Design: Susan Becker
Cover Photo: Tom Lackey

First Printing, 1998
Printed and bound in Canada by Métrolitho

This book is for
Gerald F. Wilson
who was there in the beginning
and for Penelope C. Smith
whose family helped me start again

The practice of an art
is to convert all terms
into the terms of art.

~

DONALD DAVIE

CONTENTS

Part I ~

Part II ~

Part III ~

Part IV ~

I

The heart, it's always digging up old ground,
always wanting to give things a decent burial.

~

ROO BORSON

MAN WITHOUT MEMORY ~

Watching poplars sweep the sky
dahlias withering in a garden,
two flamingos in tableau.
I know nothing of this place
or of seasons.

When you enter the room I forget
the world outside. I check
my watch; I have been awake
two minutes and must write
it down. You are the first
person I have ever seen,
ever held, ever spoken to.

You produce a diary and a pen.
In the book are entries
by my hand, but I did not write
them; I have never seen this book
before, never written a single word
anywhere.

You press me on the penmanship
which we both recognize,
and I reiterate, to distraction:
I have never seen the book before.
I have never seen you before this moment.
I know nothing of nurses or illness.

I check my watch: I have been awake
two minutes. I don't remember
your arrival. Before me
is a deck of cards laid out on a bed.
Someone is playing Patience.

Again you ask about the journal,
lined with scores of music.
This enrages me for I have never
written or conducted though you
assure me once I sang. I know
nothing of song or supplication.

I check my watch against yours: I have
been awake for only two minutes;
I have just been born: Hello
Hello, I love you.

AFTER THE FALL ~

I didn't know my house
when they sent me home.
I'd forgotten the kids' names
and couldn't shave
or cut my nails.

Geraldine, who battled
my coma and paralysis,
anger and violence,
said she found me funny
while I considered myself
disgusting and pitiful,
sitting on the loo
preparing for a bath.

DAY PATIENT ~

I won't talk
to my therapists
about the end
of sexuality.
They are women
and I am
happily married.

My wife is a teacher,
so there will be plenty
to study and learn,
plenty to discuss
in the coming years.

PUBLIC NOTICE ~

At the Holbrook Pavilion
there are the broken
the crippled
the amputated

the foreign
the lost
the non-believers

the confused
the desperate
the eroded

the blinded
the helpless
the enraged

the wishers
the dreamers
the non-dreamers

those with family
those alone
those without memory.

They're taxpayers
they're voters
they are all citizens.

Come by for a visit
if you happen
to think of it —

you won't be missed
otherwise.

CHEDOKE ~

At the end of
group therapy
Florin whipped his binder
against the wall
forgetting about pictures
from Romania

His parents and sister
knew nothing
of his escape
through Hungary
to Canada

They knew everything
regarding life beside
the Soviet Union

Florin stayed in
a home for the elderly
after his head injury
He's too well now
to reappear there

Neither has he suffered
enough to go home
though he yearns
for his family
who are further
away than the moon

which is as far
from this hospital
as only he
could wish

PUBERTY ~

My condition and age
do not permit me
to love the scent
of your perfume
and hairspray.

When you are older
you may see it
differently,
breathe it
as the rest of us do,
smell it
as you cannot now,
trying to be everything
you are not yet.

BENI'S ~

A toucan hangs
from a wooden palm

Rigid as parrots
in the window

Lifeless as swordfish
on the wall

Stiff as the patrons
at Last Call

MORNING BETTER SPENT IN BED ~

A helicopter rattles across the sky.
My Keeshond leaps to the window.
The yard is full of pale robins,
the swimming pool empty.
Mr. Italian prunes his roses.
An elderly woman hobbles by.
A Malamute howls one street over
while cicadas die in the grass.
The maple on my front lawn
dances like a shaman.
A baby cries in a buggy,
its mother a baby herself.
A crew arrives to clean the sewer,
a salesman knocks at the door.
The chopper buzzes the house again;
my little dog whines and whines.

MOUNTAIN BROW ~

Traffic above and below
the brow, business and domestic
routes. Laundry steam rises
over parked vehicles
at Henderson Hospital
before a sign reading Maternity
Departures For Admitting
Use Emergency.

Trains provide rhythm
for a walk in balance
with a dog trotting
underfoot toward autumn.

Nazi Punks Fuck Off
painted on the fence
near a stairway.

The church's cross
at Cliff Avenue
comes on at midnight, outshining
an owl-eye moon: a predator
proclaiming Hallelujah!

END OF OCTOBER ~

A cloud the shape of Australia
drifts across the moon

The sky darkened by an island
A continent

Below the lip of the mountain
a necropolis of stars

Overhead
the distant wrath of Mars

the trees so suddenly bare

II

. . .when you fail in poetry
you fail in life,
and when you fail life
you were never born
no matter what the statistics
or what your mother named you.

~

CHARLES BUKOWSKI

REALIZATION ~

I am a different man
One who died
and was reborn
A boy man
Haunted by childhood
A survivor
A wiry man
Full of rage
One with little choice
Wrestling demons
Welded to irony
A kid minus a father
A guy without dreams
A hermit
A hobbit
A hungry man
Cornered, imprisoned, beaten
A fearful man
A lost soul
Plagued by personalities
A living blank
Humiliated but stubborn
A disregarded man
A walker, a dancer, a runner
An impatient man
A merciless victim
A religious man
A singer of the heart
A silent man
A watcher
A listener

An indignant man
A labeled man
Buried alive
A Neanderthal
An android
A metaphorical man
A disabled man
A violent man
A dictator at war with wisdom
A man condemned to victory

GRIEF ENNOBLES THE MIND ~ PROUST

Four elements rose
against us in the beginning.
Custody of the children,
Julia's cancer.
My mental illness,
and severe injury.

Our parents were handfuls.
Their provinces spilled over
across our escape.
Housing here was poor.
The landlord owned a Jaguar,
his mother a Cadillac.

You won your daughters.
I stayed at home
during the chemotherapy.
My illness from childhood;
the abuse deranged me.
The person I became
in those spells was killed
in his suicide attempt.

You've seen only omens
since our union on the coast;
you pay endlessly
for your new freedom —
the family we wanted
never born.

DECLARATION ~

This is a song of hate
I am growing stronger
Rapidly in wrath
Yellow alert
Prepare for war
You will not know
I am coming
I'm learning again to keep
pain to myself
A tortured innocent
No one heard it
from me
You were safe
But you destroyed my love
Your distance is no relief
I'm shackled to your genes
I tried running from blood
The nightmare began
decades ago
I know something about
the world of dreams
The other side of life
There was no ascension
in my rebirth
Speared for years
I am a hound of hell
galloping delightfully home

PRAYER ~

How do I beg
for a silent pardon
Surely frustration
and despair were expected
My heart is wrapped
in broken glass but
I've made it this far
Am I to be laced
with horror all my life
Slower than a sloth
I cannot be a threat
Once I looked forward
to grandfatherhood
Do you require
a deeper story
I plead guilty
I've earned my shame
I owe my demoralized ally
She gave birth
to what I'm becoming
Raised me properly
in a second childhood
I cry out
in a robe she purchased
for this pilgrimage
Teach me how to fly
My eyes are wide open
and I am still flapping

AGING ~

Eat carrots
Quit smoking
Practise T'ai Chi
Listen to Mozart
Follow sports
Ride a bicycle
Walk the dogs
Forget inheritance
Return to prayer
Fear no darkness
Read the classics
Work on the house
Give up on love
Learn to relax
Plant a garden
Feed the birds
Sleep when able
Plan to make plans
Remember laughter

PENANCE ~

My obliterated childhood
undermined yours.
The abused become
abusers
generation
after generation.
Condemned for life
I scarred you
with betrayal,
you the innocent
one I once was.

SEPARATION ~

She comes to my place
bringing cream
for morning coffee,
showers occasionally
behind the striped curtain
she installed.
Painted this apartment
with her boss
before my move.
Provided a telephone
TV and microwave
to make life
manageable.
Monitors my medications,
angry with doctors for not
getting it right.
Does my laundry
in the house we own,
where I did hers
throughout the marriage.

PERSPECTIVE ~

Joy always to see you,
and sadness for life
we cannot live.
Didn't know I was
a bad guest in our
second beginning.
So frightened
I grew angry,
but meant every kiss
between tantrums.

JOEY ~

Ahh, the single-beaked robin
rescued from nature
eats hamburger
easily provided.

The simplicity of essentials.
The choice between worms
and a lean trade-off.

Its new mother
motivated by options.

PHOTOGRAPH ~

Julia was ill.
She had no strength
to face the camera. You held
her on your lap;
she could only squint
at the weeds. Jillian

beside you with the new
puppy, resembled a mother hiding
her orthodontal work.

Jessica, a pre-teen crouching
for the pose, looked through
the lens covering
her bathing suit. Her right shoulder
a skull waiting for Hallowe'en.

Between the girls your approval cloaked
by hair the way you wore it.

This is a glimpse of yesterday,
a momentary attempt to smile.

III

The difference between the right word
and the almost right word
is the difference between lightning
and the lightning bug.

~

MARK TWAIN

SURVIVOR ~

A priest says I'm brave,
but I wasn't strong
enough to let go.
It took this injury
to divide us.
That's how much
I love you.

A mute singer,
I remain
a man of words.

Forgive me
for not dying
completely.

WORDS ~

Through you
I overcame
part of what
I am,
and where
I came from.
I pray for you
every day.

Tossed my work away,
choosing the wrong
way to drown.

These words
are for you,
raked ice
between us.

ESTRANGEMENT ~

I'll be packed and ready
to go when you return
from Florida. The ceiling will be
finished, the pets and plants
cared for. I hope the children
are well after Disney World.

The house is as good
as I can leave it.
At least it's better
than when I was lost.

The bad years
never went away.
Scars in my soul
you mended until
your heart became broken.

May this holiday
be what you need.
Happy Christmas
from a man
you haven't met.

COLD WAR ~

I felt no need
for Meals on Wheels
or special transportation,
and never expected
a spell-check machine
for this disabled
man's independence.

It is a bitter thing
to be exiled
from home.

Answering the phone
and the door now
hoping for a friend,
shows my healing.

Wrong numbers
no longer intrude.
I mean to respond
in case it's you
while it still matters.

EPITAPH ~

She killed his dog.
Delivered her to the pound
where news of the breed
was not good.
When their masters leave,
there's no dealing
with that spiral
into dementia.

It was worse handling
her husband's realities.
She took longer getting
rid of the pure-bred,
so much alike
the two beasts were.

WOUNDED ~

I wish I could remember
your embrace
and being told to move
while they bruised my
limp toes and fingers.

You believed I heard you
despite the coma.
Threatened with intimacy,
eventually I obeyed.

When you reported
my parents were coming
I shocked the nurses,
sitting up punching the bed.
They feared a heart-attack;
all you could see
was my fury.

Transgression
ambushed my boyhood
throughout this town.
Survival makes me
one of many casualties
in a concealed war.

'TIL DEATH DO US PART ~

When I emerged
from my coma,
a hologram
of her husband,
I couldn't find her
though I relearned
her name.

Neither could she
reach me,
for part of her
had fallen
down those stairs
into that concrete,
a dimension no one
returns from
entirely.

AT THE GENERAL ~

I thought I'd lost her,
and cried all day, tied
to a wheelchair, facing
the wall. Nobody tried
to convince me otherwise.
I could not consider who
I was or what had occurred.

When Geraldine arrived,
she was infuriated
by my suffering,
and had it out
with the staff.
"People like him
don't know reality,"
they responded.

Nana passed in this
same hospital. She appeared
during my coma to tell me
it wasn't my time.

Living alone
two years later:
the family needs a break.

I lost more than mobility:
our children, our home, my job,
even the dogs.
Everything including
my fear of being born.

THE AFTERLIFE ~

It's the aftermath
of child abuse
A severe head injury
Love's destruction
It's losing a spiritual mate
Sobbing tear-ducts dry
Remorse and hatred
Living dead
It's abandonment
Sleeping in a bed
once shared
It's reoccurring dreams
of a grass widow wife
Counting the months
not knowing days of the week
Watching seasons come and go
Never seeing the children
It's a crazy Keeshond
who had to be put down
It's a dormant telephone
and Mormons at the door
It's life on welfare
and disability pension
Smoking tobacco again
It's Tegratal for seizures
and Prozac for depression
Waiting on the law
Returning to prayer
Keeping promises to God
and Geraldine

It's no longer asking
about reunion
It's not maybe someday
It's letting her go
alone in a journey
toward sanity

DISREGARD PREVIOUS DISPATCH ~

I return to my apartment
thinking I must record
another message on
the College number
you gave me.

I heard you've been away,
you a dream
I would not embrace.
My demons died
with who I used to be.

I rescued you from
your children's father,
but you could not
save me from my own.

Sober and healthy
in my recovery,
you intuitively understood
me, though perhaps not
my love.
Bereavement
part of the étude
in this studio.

GLADSTONE AVENUE ~

Soon I am to sleep.
Soon I will be dream-deaf
to my neighbour's return
and to the ease
in her climb
of the neglected stairs
accompanied by one
who will emerge
further sated
or deluded
having spent another night.

I will wake
having missed
their habitual
comings and goings,
their murmuring
to each other
the walls half let me hear,
and take comfort
in the silence
of all who lived here
before us.

IV

It is one thing to feel oneself in conflict
with socially sanctioned conventions,
but quite another to feel at odds
with the very root and ground of life,
with the Absolute itself.

~

ALAN W. WATTS

SCORPIO ~

I would have you know
the injury multiplied
my neuroses. Paranoia
dominates. My extremities
always unclean.

How more safely can we proceed
than by simply exchanging mail?
I stand on a mountain longing
for light from your city
across Lake Ontario.

I too am cautious. Brain-
damaged, there's nothing wrong
with my heart. I tread
slowly before the immediate
and the possible. A voice
to hear, a hand to hold.

RESOLUTION ~

I wasn't going to Heaven,
and saw no light
through a tunnel
in my coma.

Goblins of incest
watched us gleefully
while we attempted
to over-ride them.

You and I were defeated
by my drunken tumble
down illegal stairs
the day Dr. Singh
induced my recall
with his truth-serum.

The stairs were replaced
to avoid the law.
Needing to disappear,
I came this direction
for assimilation.

REHABILITATION ~

My fourth year
finds me employed
as a babysitter
in Toronto.

Wrote an old friend
when I was between
hospitals.
Hadn't seen her
in nine years,
and had no idea
what I was saying.

Her house needs upkeep,
and I need a purpose.
It gets me away
from Hamilton
and my broken life.

I have returned
to the working world,
and am finding myself
as Geraldine wanted.
My forced retirement
finally finished.

FATE ~

The man who rescued you
from your daughters' father
is still alive.
You married him
for the right reasons.
Had him leave
for the same.

Rational now in solitude,
guilt sucks him down
like quicksand
in a swirling swamp
of regrets.

Once your little hero,
if he died tomorrow
he would choose to become
your guardian angel,
if choices
are to be made.

He waits to hear
love is over
as you
would never say.
He waits to feel
his old
slanderous
heart.

G.H.B. ~

We married to save
the girls from John.
Glad we did this,
friend.
I failed you, though
it was not my fault.

My history had power
over me and my love
for you.
I will never ask
about coming home
again.
There was too much
of my father
in me.

He perished in
my near-fatal
accident.
He took you from me
long before this.

I can hardly speak
or write your name
anymore,
so far away
you are now.

DEAR JOHN ~

I still send your daughters
birthday and Christmas gifts
I'm more of a father
in my absence
than you ever were
They and their mother
know this despite
what I put them through
Waived responsibilities
Those genes
you passed on
Me I owe
the whole brood
All that's tangible
And more

CONTINUUM ~

Stopped waiting to hear
from my second wife
She will always see me
brain-injured
I am too disabled
for love
Was before the concrete
hit my head
I could make babies but
have never dealt well
with intimacy
Darwin said adapt or die
I've learned to walk lightly
and hope for the best

HYPOTHETICAL FIFTH YEAR ~

Dreaming of Alsatians
I'm jolted into high gear
by another fight upstairs.
On the radio a glitch
in welfare computers.
The money will be delayed.
I drink an instant coffee,
shave quickly, and run
around the corner
to my sister's before
the contractors return
to repair her house.
Penny makes cappuccinos then
taking my face in her hands
tries to slow me down.

Later I play Vivaldi and crank
the volume, knowing the tenants
above wonder how I landed
here, among the living.

HERMIT ~

I died as a man
and have no way
of knowing if I've come
back at all for
I am shut down
No bitterness here, only
an occurrence that made me
an alien in this world

I do not desire pity
or deserve it
I wish my wife
a clear conscience
through the years

EXPECTATIONS ~

It has been a long
hibernation
I was broken
beyond thought
My soul still

I think only of
the Panasonic remote
Another cigarette
Pens or pencils
Chewable Vitamin-C

I wait only for
Musgrave's next book
The Stanley Cup
My time in court
Things I knew before
this lumbering-slumber
I have yet
to waken from

The trick has been to
expect the unexpected
like a boy-scout
forgotten by the pack

FORTY ~

I now attend
T'ai Chi Ch'uan classes
The spine, lungs, and thighs
need the work

I practise rising
above the ashes
of life
with Geraldine

It was a long climb
out of a dry well
carrying *battered wings*
that *still kick up dust*

This is the end
of my beginning
The beginning
of another end

HARD KNOCKS ~

Here is a troubadour
suddenly middle-aged
caught in evasive maneuvers
throughout a reluctant passage

His mission a voyage
he must undertake
to reconstruct himself

He is not who he was
or
who he will become
on an exalted journey
toward another degree

That wedding band
on his night-stand

one memory in gold

ACKNOWLEDGMENTS

Athabasca University Magazine published an early version of Gladstone Avenue. Other poems were published by *Tidepool, Beneath the Surface, paperplates*, and *i.e. Magazine (information and education that is about brain injury).*

Twenty-five of these poems were published as a chapbook entitled *The Afterlife* by Hamilton Haiku Press (Herb Barrett), 1992.

Fate, G.H.B., Forty, and Hard Knocks were published in a pamphlet entitled *Fate* by Cactus Tree Press, 1995.

Man Without Memory, Declaration, Prayer, Survivor, The Afterlife, Resolution, Forty and Continuum appeared in *Understatement, An Anthology of Twelve Poets* by Seraphim Editions, 1996.

The italicized lines in Forty are borrowed from "Only Us" by Peter Gabriel.

A special thanks to:
Dr. Alison Kelford Smith
Gérard Dion
Karen Marshall
Julie Whittaker
Susan Walker
Jean Baird
Ken Puley
Bernard Kelly

Born and raised in Hamilton, Ontario, Robert Boates now lives in Toronto. His previous publications include *The Good Life* (a work in progress). In 1986, he shared first place in a national poetry competition, sponsored by Fame Canada Enterprises, of Victoria, B.C. An actor and childcare worker, Boates survived a brain injury sustained in 1989. Through poetry, he prevails, in an arena of chaos.